How To Help Someone With Dementia

The Ultimate Guide on How To Deal With a Parent With Dementia And Others

Edward Katherine

Copyright © by **Edward Katherine**

All rights reserved. No part of this publication may be reproduced, distributed, or transmitted in any form or by any means, including photocopying, recording, or other electronic or mechanical methods, without the prior written permission of the publisher, except in the case of brief quotations embodied in critical reviews and certain other noncommercial uses permitted by copyright law.

Table of Contents

Chapter 1

Understanding Dementia

Dementia is a broad term for severe memory, language, problem-solving, and other cognitive impairments that interfere with daily life.

Dementia is not one illness. It is a broad phrase used to describe a set of symptoms that people may encounter if they have a range of conditions, including Alzheimer's disease. Disorders categorized as "dementia" are brought on by abnormal changes in the brain. Dementia symptoms cause a significant deterioration in thinking capabilities, also known as cognitive capacities, that impair daily life and independent function. They also influence behavior, emotions, and relationships.

Alzheimer's disease accounts for 60–80% of cases. Vascular dementia, caused by microscopic bleeding and blood artery obstruction in the brain, is the second most frequent type of dementia. Mixed dementia occurs when multiple types of dementia cause brain abnormalities at the same time. There are numerous other illnesses that can produce cognitive impairment but are not dementia, some of which are treatable, such as thyroid disorders and vitamin shortages.

The term "senility" or "senile dementia," which is often used incorrectly to refer to dementia, is a reflection of the once-common but false belief that significant mental decline is a typical part of aging.

Dementia is not a disease; rather, it refers to a set of symptoms that affect the brain. Dementia can be classified into numerous categories based on the cause. Knowing what type of dementia you have allows you to receive treatment that is better tailored to your needs.

The most prevalent types of dementia are:

Alzheimer's disease.
Alzheimer's disease is a type of dementia that affects the area of the brain that controls memory, language, and thought. Alzheimer's and dementia are frequently confused with one another, which can create distress and confusion.

Vascular Dementia
Vascular dementia is the second most frequent kind of dementia, following Alzheimer's disease. This type of dementia occurs when the brain is injured due to a lack of blood supply, such as after a stroke.

Different types of dementia
There are also other kinds of dementia, including dementia with Lewy bodies and frontotemporal dementia. Parkinson's disease and Huntington's disease can cause specific types of dementia.

The many distinct varieties of dementia and related illnesses might be bewildering for someone who has been diagnosed with dementia or knows someone who has.

Symptoms and indications of dementia.

The symptoms of dementia might vary widely. Examples include issues with:

- *Short-term memory.*
- *Keeping track of your handbag or money.*
- *Paying bills.*
- *Planning and preparing meals.*
- *Remembering appointments.*
- *Traveling outside of the neighborhood.*

The symptoms of cognitive impairment gradually develop over time, eventually leading to dementia, as dementia is a degenerative condition. If someone you know is having memory problems or other changes in their cognitive skills, don't dismiss them. Consult a doctor quickly to determine the cause. Professional evaluation may reveal a curable illness. Even if symptoms suggest dementia, early diagnosis allows a person to get the most out of existing therapies and gives them the opportunity to participate in clinical trials or studies, it also allows time to plan for the future.

Chapter 2

Communicating Effectively

We are not born knowing how to communicate with those who have dementia, but we can learn. Improving your communication skills will reduce the burden of caregiving and most likely increase the quality of your relationship with your loved one. Good communication skills will also help you deal with unpleasant behavior that may arise when caring for someone with dementia.

Set a pleasant tone for interaction

Your attitude and body language. Your sentiments and thoughts are communicated more effectively than your words. Set a positive tone by communicating with your loved one in a polite and courteous manner. Use facial expressions, tone of speech, and physical touch to convey your message and demonstrate affection.

Get the individual's attention

Reduce distractions and noise by turning off the radio or television, closing the curtains or door, or moving to a quieter environment. Make sure she is paying attention before you talk; utilize nonverbal cues and touch to keep her interested. Address her by name. Introduce yourself. If she's seated, go down to her level and maintain eye contact.

Express your message clearly

Use simple vocabulary and sentences. Speak in a soothing tone, slowly, and with clarity. Avoid increasing or loudening your voice; instead, reduce it. If she doesn't get it the first time, use the same words to restate your message or query. Wait a few minutes and try again with a different question if she's still not understanding. Use names of individuals and places instead of pronouns or abbreviations.

Ask basic, answerable questions

Ask one question at a time; yes/no answers work best. Avoid asking open-ended questions or presenting too many options. For example, inquire, "Would you like to wear your white shirt or your blue shirt? Better still, show her the options; visual aids and cues can assist clarify your inquiry and direct her response.

Listen with your eyes, ears, and emotions

Be patient as you wait for your loved one's reply. If she is having trouble coming up with an answer, it is acceptable to make suggestions. Look for nonverbal signs and body language, and respond appropriately. Always endeavor to listen for the meaning and emotions behind the words.

Break down actions into a set of steps

This makes many chores far more manageable. You can support your loved one in doing what he can, aid him with tasks he can no longer complete on his own, and gently remind him of steps he frequently forgets to take. Visual cues, such as indicating to him with your hand where to set the meal plate, can be really useful.

When the going gets rough, divert and redirect

If your loved one becomes irritated or agitated, consider changing the topic or setting. For example, ask him for assistance or suggest going for a walk. Before redirecting, make an emotional connection with the person. You may say, "I see you're sad; I'm sorry you're angry. Let's grab something to eat.

Respond with warmth and comfort

Dementia patients frequently report feeling confused, worried, and unsure of themselves. Furthermore, people frequently lose track of reality and recollect events that did not actually occur. Avoid trying to persuade them that they are wrong. Maintain your focus on the sentiments they are expressing (which are genuine), and respond with verbal and physical displays of comfort, support, and assurance. When everything else fails, holding hands, touching, hugging, and praising the person can help get them to respond.

Remember those good old days
Remembering the past is frequently a relaxing and encouraging exercise. Many persons with dementia may not remember what happened a half-hour ago, yet they can vividly recall their lives thirty-five years prior. As a result, avoid asking inquiries that rely on short-term recall, such as what the person ate for lunch. Instead, ask general inquiries about the individual's distant past; this knowledge is more likely to be remembered.

Maintain a sense of humor
Use humor whenever feasible, but not at the person's expense. People with dementia often retain their social abilities and enjoy laughing with you.

Chapter 3

Creating a Supportive Environment

As the condition advances, it is critical to create a dementia-friendly atmosphere that fosters comfort, safety, and a sense of belonging. If your loved one has memory loss or struggles to learn new things, they may forget they are in their own home, where things are, and how household goods work.

This article will look at how to build a dementia-friendly environment, as well as how our dementia caregivers can make your loved one's home more accessible and familiar to them.

A dementia-friendly setting is a living place that has been carefully constructed, both physically and socially, to fulfill the needs of a person with dementia.

The area tries to alleviate uncertainty, anxiety, and disorientation by creating a helpful and comforting environment for them. Making minor changes to a living space can dramatically improve the quality of life for loved ones with dementia or other dementia-related diseases, such as Alzheimer's disease.

Add simple signs to spots throughout the home
Clear and basic signs can be quite beneficial to those with dementia. Placing labels or signs on doors, drawers, and cupboards can help you find important goods and navigate through your home.

Use contrasting colors and large, easy-to-read typefaces to increase visibility. Putting up one-word signs or graphics, such as BEDROOM, KITCHEN, or TOILET, with arrows pointing to those rooms will assist them avoid becoming lost. These visual clues create a sense of familiarity, allowing your loved one to remain independent in their own home for longer.

Declutter to make objects more accessible

Excessive clutter can confound and overwhelm people with dementia, causing tension and frustration.

It is critical to organize your loved one's stuff, remove unneeded items, and make sure that regularly used objects are conveniently accessible around their home. By reducing their living area, people might feel more at ease and in control.

Reduce the undesirable background noise

Individuals with dementia may find background noise extremely distracting and unpleasant. Laminated and tiled flooring, rugs, and drapes help absorb background noise, making it less stressful for them.

Reduce noise levels by keeping the television or radio at a reasonable volume and minimizing outside noise. Consider employing gentle, soothing music to create a relaxing atmosphere. By eliminating aural distractions, your loved one will be able to focus better and enjoy a more calm environment.

Include photos to spark recollections

Photographs have high emotional significance and can act as powerful memory triggers. Displaying familiar images throughout the home can trigger memories, spark conversations, and foster a sense of belonging.

Choose important images from different periods of your loved one's life and display them prominently, such as in the living room or bedroom. These visual reminders assist individuals with dementia in connecting with their own past and maintaining a feeling of identity.

Feature more simple to grasp

As dementia progresses, people may have difficulty recognizing the purpose and usage of daily home items.

Consider replacing sophisticated equipment or gadgets with simpler options that come with straightforward instructions. Using large-button telephones, easy-to-read clocks, or color-coded kitchen utensils, for example, can increase independence while decreasing frustration. Adapting the environment to your loved one's cognitive capacities increases their sense of autonomy and confidence.

Chapter 4

Managing Daily Activities

Not everyone will struggle with all of these activities, and a person's symptoms may progress at varying speeds. The following information describes how dementia typically impacts daily tasks.

Using the Toilet

People with dementia may have difficulty using the toilet. Some persons may have difficulty getting to the toilet on time due to coordination and movement issues. Some people might forget where the bathroom is. Incontinence is prevalent in the latter stages of dementia, and people will require extensive practical care to manage it.

Bathing

As someone's dementia worsens, they will require more assistance with washing and bathing. To begin, someone may need to be reminded to take a bath or wash their hair. People suffering from dementia will eventually require complete assistance with their personal care routines including laundry.

Getting dressed

A person with dementia may struggle to dress themselves and require assistance with items such as buttons and shoelaces. As dementia worsens, it may be helpful to receive help choosing clothes and putting them on so that they are comfortable and positioned correctly.

Eating

People with dementia may struggle to chew and swallow, use utensils, and change their dietary preferences over time. In the late stages of dementia, persons may require assistance from loved ones or caregivers to eat.

Preparing food and beverages

Following a procedure, such as making a hot drink or preparing a meal, are complex tasks that grow more difficult for people with dementia. Providing support at mealtimes can help people remember to eat all of their meals and acquire enough nutrients from their food. In the later stages of dementia, patients frequently require drinks and meals prepared for them to ensure they are eating as well as possible.

Taking medicine

Many people struggle to remember to take their medications, but people with dementia typically have a tougher time doing so. Some people find it handy to keep their medication in a box labeled with the time and day to help them keep track. As dementia worsens, patients may require assistance with taking their medications.

Housework

People with dementia may require assistance with household tasks. Over time, individuals may find it increasingly difficult to use a vacuum cleaner, or they may begin a domestic job and become overwhelmed, forcing them to stop. As keeping the house clean and neat becomes more challenging, additional assistance from carers or loved ones is sometimes required to do these activities.

Shopping

Shopping can be more challenging for those with dementia. They may forget the products they came out for, become disoriented in a store if things have changed around, or discover that counting change at the till takes longer. As their dementia worsens, they will require additional assistance from others to complete their shopping.

Keeping appointments

Keeping track of appointments and social activities can be challenging for someone with dementia as their memory and reasoning skills deteriorate over time. It can be beneficial to keep a pen and notebook near the phone to record dates and locations, as well as to have reminders on a calendar on the door or to have a loved one assist the person in keeping track of their appointments in the later stages of the condition.

Managing finances

Managing money, paying bills on time, and staying on top of finances can be challenging and burdensome for someone living with dementia. This can be difficult, even in the early stages of dementia. People may find it beneficial to have a financial counselor to assist them, but many people prefer to get a Lasting Power of Attorney to manage their affairs on their behalf.

Using technology

Many routine chores, including banking, shopping, and staying in touch with others, require the use of the Internet or other technological tools. People with dementia may find it difficult to use computers, web pages, and apps. People with dementia may need assistance from others to use some gadgets, even basic ones like alarm clocks, as their condition worsens.

Talking with people

Some people may struggle to remember the meanings of certain words, while others may take their time finding the appropriate term when speaking. This can mean that, while people can handle most parts of everyday living on their own, they may struggle to maintain a conversation. People in the final stages of dementia may rarely talk, and friends and family frequently create alternative ways of communicating with them that are comforting.

Using the Telephone

People with dementia may struggle to use the phone and become confused about phone numbers. Dementia patients may begin to forget familiar phone numbers or how to utilize an answer phone. Simple mobile phones, call screening services, and phones with larger buttons can be beneficial. Some people may feel more at ease allowing a loved one to use the phone on their behalf in the later stages of the condition.

Walking

To begin with, someone with dementia may not require physical assistance while walking; however, some varieties of dementia might induce alterations in a person's walking or balance early on. Initially, walkers or sticks may be required just when away from home, but mobility at home can deteriorate over time. People may eventually need a lot of assistance walking or moving from a bed to a chair. Some individuals will need to utilize a wheelchair.

Driving

Driving can provide a great deal of independence, but because dementia impairs thinking, reasoning, and responses, most people eventually be forced to cease driving. Some persons may be qualified for a medical assessment to determine whether they can continue to drive. When someone is diagnosed with dementia, they must notify the Driver and Vehicle Licensing Agency (DVLA). To get to the grocery store or an appointment, a person suffering from dementia might need to rely on family members or the public transit system.

Using public transportation

Using public transportation, such as a bus or train, can help people with dementia go around and maintain their independence. People may want additional assistance to remember routes and timetables. As dementia progresses, people may prefer to stay closer to home and travel only when accompanied by others.

Finding Your Way

Dementia can impair a person's ability to remember street names or follow directions from a map. This means that people can easily become confused or disoriented, even in familiar surroundings. As dementia progresses, people may prefer to go out with a loved one or caregiver so that they do not feel lost or disoriented while away from home.

Watching Television

Because dementia impairs memory and focus, people may struggle to follow plot lines or remember character names when watching television. Many individuals with dementia continue to enjoy watching television, but with time, they may be unable to recollect everything they have seen and may no longer be interested in the same topics they once were.

Reading

Many people with dementia enjoy reading, but as their condition worsens, they may struggle to follow lines of text or remember chunks of literature. A person in the late stages of dementia may be unable or unwilling to read but would prefer to have someone read to them or listen to an audiobook.

Chapter 5

Nurturing Emotional Wellbeing

Dementia might cause your senior loved ones to say strange things or become confused while out in public. As they awkwardly interact with business owners, neighbors, or even total strangers, you could feel humiliated.

It can be distressing to deal with loved ones displaying behavior associated with dementia, both in private and in public. The tips below can help you manage tough encounters caused by your senior's illness:

Seniors who have dementia may struggle to distinguish between truth and memory or imagination. Correcting seniors with dementia might increase bewilderment, tension, worry, or even wrath, exacerbating dementia symptoms.

When feasible, experts recommend affirming and joining your loved one's reality. If your senior occasionally speaks as if they are living in the past, continue the conversation without correcting them as long as it does not cause them harm. Let it go, for instance, if your senior believes it's Monday when it's actually Friday. There's no need to correct them. Use distractions and diversions.

Experts recommend employing situational distractions to assist dementia patients remain calm and avoid worsening symptoms. For example, if telling your senior that you are taking them for a medical examination causes them distress, you may tell them that you are going to the park and will make a stop on the way home to see a doctor.

You may also choose to distract your senior from stressful issues or if you see they are constantly repeating themselves. Changing the subject to the weather or asking them for help with a basic activity can help to calm the atmosphere.

Some people may feel guilty about employing therapeutic distractions or diversions, which is entirely acceptable. Just remember that the idea is to make your loved one feel at ease while also finding a balance that works for both of you. Provide brief explanations and moderate corrections.

Sometimes you have to correct a senior who is confused. In cases like this, keep it as gentle and brief as possible. Reduce uncertainty and bad feelings by framing your corrections as ideas. You might say, "Why don't we go for a walk together?" as an example rather than saying, "I can't let you go outside alone because you might fall or get lost."

Make sure you utilize basic terms and phrases that your loved one will understand. Physical reminders, such as images, might also be useful in gradually reorienting a senior with dementia as needed. Respond to sensations, not words.

Consider what emotion might be behind your loved one's comments. If they are lashing out, it could be because they are terrified. In this scenario, you can tell them that everything is well and maybe give them a hug or hold their hand. Always have a cool demeanor when responding.

Chapter 6

Managing Challenging Behaviors

One of the most difficult aspects of caring for a loved one with Alzheimer's or any dementia is dealing with the problematic behavior and personality changes that frequently occur. Aggression, hallucinations, roaming, and eating or sleeping troubles all be distressing and complicate your duty as a caretaker. Whatever issues you're facing, keep in mind that the person with dementia isn't trying to be difficult. Often, your loved one's behavioral troubles are exacerbated by their surroundings, inability to cope with stress, or frustrated attempts to communicate.

By making a few easy modifications, you may reduce your loved one's stress, better manage their symptoms, and greatly improve both their well-being and your own caregiving experience. The first step in treating bothersome behavior is to determine why your patient is stressed or what is causing them discomfort.

As you try to determine the causes, keep in mind that a patient with dementia responds far more to your facial expression, tone of voice, and body language than to the words you speak. So, utilize eye contact, a smile, or a soothing touch to deliver your message and demonstrate compassion. And, rather than taking bad behaviors personally, try to maintain a sense of humor.

Identifying Common Causes of Problem Behavior

Consider your loved one's body language and envision what they are feeling or trying to say.

Consider what occurred immediately prior to the onset of the problematic behavior. Did something cause the behavior? Common triggers include being in strange circumstances or struggling with chores or communication. These events can leave your loved one feeling helpless or bewildered, resulting in anger.

Is the patient's need being met? Is your loved one experiencing hunger, thirst, or pain? Physical discomforts, such as being exposed to loud noises or a frenetic environment, can generate anxiety and lead to behavioral issues.

Does changing the atmosphere, such as playing the person's favorite music, make them feel better?

How did you respond to the problematic behavior? Did your reaction help to calm the patient, or did it worsen the behavior? Is your stress causing the behavior problems?

Create a peaceful and pleasant environment.
The setting and ambiance you create when caring for an Alzheimer's or dementia patient can have a significant impact on their sense of peace and safety.

Modify the environment to eliminate potential stresses that cause agitation and disorientation. Loud or incomprehensible noises, dark lighting, mirrors or other reflecting surfaces, gaudy colors, and patterned wallpaper are among examples.

Maintain your own inner peace. Getting anxious or irritated in response to bad behavior can exacerbate the patient's stress. Respond to the emotion conveyed by the conduct, not to the behavior itself. Try to stay flexible, patient, and easygoing. If you feel yourself becoming worried or losing control, take a break to calm down.

Manage stress in Alzheimer's or dementia patients.
Some stress-reduction tactics are more effective for Alzheimer's patients than others, so you may need to experiment to find the ones that work best for your loved one.

Exercise is a great stress reliever for both the Alzheimer's sufferer and you as the caregiver. Regular walking, dancing, or sitting activities help improve a variety of behavioral behaviors, including aggression, roaming, and difficulties sleeping. Indoor retail malls provide many strolling options while keeping you out of the elements.

Simple activities might help your loved one reconnect with their former life. Someone who once enjoyed cooking, for example, may still find enjoyment in the simple chore of washing vegetables for dinner. Try to engage your loved one in as many daily activities as possible. Folding laundry, watering plants, or taking a trip to the country can all help to relieve tension.

Remembering the past may also assist to relax and soothe your loved one. Even if they can't remember what happened a few minutes ago, they may be able to recollect events from decades before. Consider asking generic queries about their distant past.

When your loved one is anxious, play calming music or their favorite sort of music to help them relax. Mealtimes and bathtimes with an Alzheimer's patient can be made simpler for both of you by using music therapy to help calm them down.

Interaction with other people remains crucial. While big gatherings of strangers might be stressful for an Alzheimer's or dementia patient, spending time with diverse people in one-on-one settings can help to promote physical and social activity while also relieving stress.

Pets can be a source of pleasant nonverbal communication. The pleasant connection and soft touch of a well-trained, docile animal can help calm your loved one and reduce violent behavior. If you don't have your own pet, there are groups that provide pet visits to people with Alzheimer's or dementia.

Take time to truly connect with the individual you're caring for. Taking a few minutes each day to truly connect with your loved one can trigger the production of hormones that improve their mood and reduce stress. You might experience anything similar from it. Even if your loved one is no longer able to communicate vocally, it is critical that you devote some time when you are at your most peaceful to totally focus on them. Avoid distractions like the TV or phone, make eye contact whenever possible, hold their hand or touch their cheek, and speak in a calm, comforting tone of voice. When you interact in this way, you will benefit from a process that reduces stress and promotes well-being.

Wandering.

Restlessness and confusion are two common triggers for wandering. When an Alzheimer's patient is hungry, thirsty, constipated, or in pain, he or she may become agitated. Additionally, if they are bored, nervous, or stressed out due to an uncomfortable environment or not getting enough exercise, they may become disoriented, pace, or wander. In addition to increasing physical exercise in your loved one's regular routine, you can:

Pacing or restless behavior should be immediately directed toward productive activities or exercise.

Reassure the individual if they appear bewildered
Distract the person with another activity during the time of day when they are most likely to stray.

Reduce noise and confusion. Turn off the television or radio, close the curtains, or relocate the patient to a quieter environment.

Consult your doctor, as disorientation can also be caused by pharmaceutical side effects, drug interactions, or over-medicating.

Practical strategies to avoid wandering
Install child-safety equipment in your home to secure doors and windows.

Hide goods that your loved one would want if they left the house, such as handbags, shoes, or glasses.

Acquire comfy chairs that limit movement, making it difficult for the sufferer to rise up without help.

Use safety features like sensors and sirens. Bed and chair alarms can notify you if your loved one gets up and wanders. Pressure-activated floor mats and passive infrared (PIR) sensors provide similar functions, allowing you to reroute the individual before they go too far.

Plan for when your loved one wanders
If your loved one does wander, it's a good idea to have a plan in place.

Implement a medical alert system. In addition to allowing your loved one to call for help in an emergency, some versions have location monitoring technology. This is especially useful if your loved one wanders off or becomes lost in a new place.

Inform neighbors and local police about your loved one's tendency to roam, and distribute your phone number.

Have your loved one wear an ID bracelet or clothing label
In the event that a police search is required, bring a current photo of your loved one and some unwashed clothing to assist search-and-rescue dogs. Place clothing in a plastic bag while wearing gloves, and replace it once a month.

Sign up for the Alzheimer's Association's Medic Alert and Safe Return Program in the United States, which is an identification system that assists in the recovery of lost Alzheimer's patients.

How to locate a missing Alzheimer's patient.
Even when confined, a person with dementia may not call for help or respond to your calls, putting them at risk of dehydration and hypothermia. Look out for potentially dangerous areas surrounding your house, such as high balconies, bus stops, tunnels, deep vegetation, and bodies of water.

Search within a one-mile radius of where the individual in need was before wandering.

Search within one hundred feet of a road, as most wanderers begin and end their journeys there. Look carefully into shrubs and ditches, as your loved one could have fallen or become trapped.

Look in the direction of the wanderer's dominant hand. People typically travel first in their dominant direction.

Investigate familiar locations, such as past homes or favorite locales. Wandering often has a specific destination.

Rummaging and hiding objects
Caring for a patient who rummages through or hides items in the home might be difficult, but not impossible.

Protecting property.
To protect the contents of specific rooms or cabinets, lock them, and keep all valuables secure.

Have mail delivered somewhere out of your loved one's reach, such as a post office box.

If objects disappear, discover the person's preferred hiding areas.

Restrict trashcan access, and inspect all wastebaskets before disposing of their contents to ensure that no things have been hidden inside.

Keeping your loved one safe from harm
Prevent access to potentially dangerous substances like cleaning chemicals, alcohol, guns, power tools, sharp knives, and pharmaceuticals.

Block unused electrical outlets with safeguarding devices.
Hide the stove knobs so the person cannot turn on the burners.
Lower the temperature of water heaters.

Designate a particular drawer of objects for the person to safely "play" with when they want to rummage.

Anger and Aggression

While having a calm environment can have a significant impact on managing the stress that frequently leads to violent conduct, there are also things you can do during an angry episode.

Do not confront the person or attempt to address the furious conduct. Remember that a person with dementia cannot reflect on or regulate undesirable behavior.

Don't make physical contact during the outburst. This may lead to physical violence.

Allow the person to act out their aggression. Allow them to be angry alone, just make sure both of you are safe.

Distract the person with a more delightful activity.

Look for patterns of hostility. Consider variables like privacy, independence, boredom, pain, and exhaustion. Avoid activities or themes that make your loved one angry. Seek assistance from others during activities that irritate the sufferer and must be avoided. Do not take the aggression personally. It's all part of the dementia.

Hallucinations and suspicion

Hallucinations may be the result of your loved one's fading senses. Maintaining a quiet environment can help lessen the frequency of hallucinations or illusions, but if they do occur, do not quarrel about what is real and what is imagination. Instead, address the emotional content of what the individual is saying. For example, if a loved one feels terrified, provide consolation. Alternatively, you could distract your loved one by engaging in another activity or relocating to a different room.

<u>Alzheimer's and suspicion or paranoia</u>
Confusion and memory loss can lead Alzheimer's patients to grow suspicious of others around them, accusing them of stealing, treachery, or other inappropriate behavior. Violent films and television can also add to paranoia.

Provide a brief response to any charges, but don't debate or try to persuade them that their suspicions are unfounded.

<u>Distract the patient with another activity, such as taking a stroll.</u>
If suspicions of theft are centered on a specific article that is frequently misplaced, such as a wallet, keep a replica item on hand to swiftly assuage the patient's concerns.

Sleep troubles
Brain disease frequently interrupts the sleep-wake cycle. Patients with Alzheimer's disease may become awake, confused, and disoriented at dusk and throughout the night. This is called "sundowning."

There are two aspects to sundowning. First, confusion, overstimulation, and exhaustion during the day might cause restlessness at night. Second, some Alzheimer's patients develop a phobia of the dark, maybe due to the absence of familiar daytime noises and activity. To reduce their suffering, the sufferer may want security and protection at night.

<u>Tips for reducing evening restlessness.</u>
Improve your sleep hygiene. To help your loved one fall asleep, provide a comfy bed, turn down the noise and light, and play relaxing music. If they prefer to sleep on a chair or on the couch, ensure certain they cannot fall out while sleeping.

Maintain a regular sleep routine. Maintain a consistent sleep schedule and nightly routine. For example, offer the person a bath and some warm milk before bedtime.

Keep a nightlight on. Some patients with dementia get angry when they imagine things in the dark. Stuffed animals or pets may also assist the patient relax and falling asleep.

Place a commode next to the bed. Walking to the restroom in the middle of the night may wake the individual up too much, making it difficult to fall back again.

Increase your loved one's physical activity during the day to assist them feel more fatigued before bedtime.

Keep an eye on who is taking naps. If the person appears to be particularly tired during the day, a brief nap in the afternoon can help him or her sleep better that night. But keep your naps short.

Limit the patient's intake of coffee, sugar, and junk food throughout the day.

<u>Coping with nightly wakefulness and pacing</u>
If your loved one paces at night, make sure they have a safe space to do so, or have another caregiver take over. You, too, need to rest. In the late stages of Alzheimer's, you should consider a hospital bed with guardrails.

Some dementia patients have trouble falling or keeping asleep because they do not respond to day-night transitions. Increasing strong light exposure throughout the day and using melatonin tablets at night may help them sleep better.

Eating issues
It can be difficult for any caregiver to ensure that someone with Alzheimer's consumes adequate food and fluids. In addition to encouraging exercise to help your loved one feel hungrier and thirstier, consider these suggestions:

<u>Keep track of your prescriptions</u>
Some drugs impair appetite. Others may induce dry mouth, so ensure that your loved one drinks plenty of fluids while eating.

Discuss eating issues with their doctor to determine whether any
medications need to be changed.

Make mealtimes pleasant for your loved one.
Place flowers on the table or play relaxing music. Prepare your loved
one's favorite cuisine and serve it on dishes that contrast sharply
with the food's hues. Reduce distractions in the dining area and
avoid items that are overly hot or cold.

Make feeding lively, fun, and uncomplicated.
Try feeding your loved one little spoonfuls while singing humorous
rhymes. When they open their mouth to smile, drop in some food.
People with dementia may have difficulty using standard utensils, so
opt for finger foods or children's sipper cups.

Monitor chewing and swallowing.
Chewing and swallowing problems can develop as Alzheimer's
disease advances. If required, instruct your loved one on when to
chew and swallow. After eating, keep them upright for twenty
minutes to avoid breathing difficulties.

Transition to pureed or soft foods.
In the final stages of Alzheimer's, your loved one may lose the ability
to swallow solid meals. Switch to a liquid-only diet when the time
comes.

Chapter 7

Creating a Support Network

Maintaining a strong social support network can become more difficult as people age. Some elders are unable to leave their homes as frequently as they once did due to mobility concerns. Others may feel alienated once their children and families have moved away. In fact, more than half of seniors over 60 are in danger of isolation. But how can seniors establish social support networks to sustain their quality of life?

Connect with friends and family.

As we get older, it might be more difficult to maintain relationships with friends and family. Your older loved one may feel isolated, especially if people move away or become preoccupied with their own work or family. This is why having a communication pattern is so important. It is helpful if family members work together to ensure that everyone stays in touch with an elderly loved one who lives alone. Schedule regular phone calls or Zoom sessions, and plan in-person visits whenever possible. Make sure your loved one has access to the forms of transportation required for peer socialization. If they cannot drive themselves, consider offering them a ride.

Participate in community activities.

People of all ages benefit much from being linked to their communities. From volunteering to community events, most locations offer a wide range of possibilities for seniors to engage in activities that link them with others. This gives elders a sense of purpose and success as they contribute to their community and form social connections.

Join a senior center.

Meeting others who have similar interests and concerns can be the most difficult aspect of expanding one's social network. Connecting with others at similar stages of life is an excellent approach for seniors to locate people with whom they share experiences and common ground. As a result, many older people could benefit from attending a senior center.

Senior centers provide a wide range of activities and opportunities. A senior center, which offers programs and fitness equipment, can be an excellent way to get out of the house while building new social connections.

Some need help putting themselves out there.
Even under ideal conditions, it can be difficult to form and maintain connections. Getting out and meeting people is especially tough for seniors, who frequently face transportation and mobility difficulties. Many elders may not have the same instinctive understanding of technology as younger individuals who grew up using it on a daily basis. In today's digital age, this can put seniors at a disadvantage. Seniors may struggle not only to access critical digital materials but also to navigate the social opportunities provided by the internet.

Fortunately, an in-home caregiver can assist on all of these fronts. Caregivers can assist your older loved one in maintaining contact with loved ones and discovering new possibilities for socialization. Caregivers can help your senior loved one establish their social network by providing transportation and guiding them through internet opportunities. Of course, caregivers can provide companionship and company for your loved one even when they aren't in the mood for a large social gathering. With the care and compassion that an in-home caregiver provides, your loved one will be able to expand their social circle and enjoy all that life in their golden years has to offer.

Chapter 8

Self-care for Caregivers

It can have a significant emotional, physical, and mental impact on caregivers. Caregivers frequently overlook their own health while offering steadfast assistance to persons suffering from dementia. This article intends to highlight the significance of self-care for caregivers and provide practical techniques for navigating the hurdles while maintaining personal health.

<u>Ways to Practice Self-Care for Caregivers</u>

Physical Self-care
Physical well-being is the foundation of self-care. Adequate sleep, regular exercise, and a healthy diet are all necessary components. Physical self-care begins with establishing a consistent sleep regimen, engaging in enjoyable physical activities, and feeding the body nourishing foods.

Acknowledge your emotions
Caring for someone with dementia can generate a wide range of emotions, including love, fulfillment, frustration, and grief. It is critical that caregivers identify and validate these emotions. Seek help from friends, family, or a support group to express your emotions and experiences.

Mental and Emotional Self-Care
Caring for one's mental and emotional wellness is equally important. Mindfulness meditation, journaling, and seeking professional counseling all provide opportunities for self-reflection and emotional release. Developing resilience, stress management skills, and a positive mentality all help to improve mental and emotional well-being.

Learn to delegate

Recognize that it is OK to delegate work. Friends, relatives, or professional aid can help with specific tasks, allowing you to focus on your own needs. Delegating does not indicate weakness; rather, it is an effective approach to avoid burnout.

Take breaks and rest

Caregivers may feel terrible about taking breaks, but self-care requires time to rest and relax. To provide yourself with a break, schedule respite care. Even small getaways can restore your mind and body, allowing you to deliver better care.

Setting boundaries

Establishing and maintaining appropriate boundaries is an important part of self-care. This entails learning to say 'no' when required, acknowledging personal boundaries, and making space for oneself. Setting boundaries protects individuals' time and energy, promoting a healthier balance between personal and professional life.

Social Connections

Making and maintaining meaningful social connections is a highly effective self-care strategy. Spending time with loved ones, cultivating strong relationships, and getting help when necessary can all contribute to a sense of belonging and emotional well-being. Social relationships protect against stress and give a support system during difficult times.

Engaging in Hobbies

Pursuing hobbies and activities that bring you joy and contentment is an excellent self-care activity. Engaging in activities that match with personal interests, such as reading, drawing, gardening, or playing a musical instrument, promotes a sense of purpose and happiness.

Caregivers frequently forget to care for themselves while providing altruistic care. Recognizing the significance of self-care benefits both the caregiver and the person living with dementia. Prioritizing one's physical, emotional, and mental health allows caregivers to continue providing effective and compassionate care. Recognizing the value of self-care is both an investment in personal health and a commitment to cultivating a more balanced and satisfying life. When we emphasize self-care, we not only benefit ourselves but also help to build a healthier and more compassionate society.

Conclusion

The way a person with dementia feels and experiences life is determined by more than simply their disease. Their relationships, environment, and support all influence their experience. Caregivers, friends, and family can make a person with dementia feel valued and included.

Support should be tailored to the person as an individual. This is referred to as person-centered care. Support should also focus on improving their well-being and addressing their requirements. It's critical to focus on what the person still has, rather than what they may have lost. Concentrate on the person's feelings rather than their memories.

The person with dementia may be experiencing a world that is completely different from those around them. To understand and help the individual, attempt to perceive things from their point of view and identify their coping techniques.

Coping strategies that a person with dementia can utilize

Practical strategies.
Making ahead decisions, establishing a long-term power of attorney, or setting up triggers or reminders

Social strategies
Relying on family assistance, seeking spiritual support, and joining new activity groups

Emotional tactics
Using humor, focusing on short-term pleasure or living in the moment, and focusing on good aspects

Health Improvement Strategies
Exercising more, having a healthy diet, limiting alcohol and smoking.

Responses to Dementia

A person's reaction to dementia will be determined by their personality, previous experiences, understanding of dementia, social and emotional support, and environment. People may use various coping mechanisms at different times.

Some people may not recognize that they have dementia. They may deny that they are having difficulty. Others may be aware that things are becoming more difficult but believe this is a natural aspect of aging rather than dementia.

Understanding Denial and Lack of Insight

When someone is told they have dementia, they cannot comprehend or accept the news. This could be because the person is in denial or suffers from a 'loss of insight'.

Identity

A person's sense of identity, or how they see themselves, is influenced by a variety of things, including their connections, roles in the family and community, hobbies, and line of work. For example, someone may describe oneself as an avid gardener.

Dementia-related alterations might alter a person's sense of self. It is critical that family, friends, and caregivers are aware of this since they can impact how a person with dementia perceives themselves. They should aim to treat the person with dementia as an individual rather than defining them by the disease or focusing on negative elements like lost ability.

Behavioral changes

As dementia progresses, a person may exhibit demanding and upsetting behavior, both for themselves and those around them. A person suffering from dementia, for example, may:

- ❖ ***Become restless or agitated***
- ❖ ***Shout or scream.***

- ❖ *Get wary of others.*
- ❖ *Follow somebody around.*
- ❖ *Ask the same inquiry repeatedly.*

These out-of-character behaviors might occur when a person's demand is not met and they are unable to convey it. For example:

- ❖ **They may be thirsty, hungry, or experiencing discomfort.**
- ❖ **They could have misconstrued something and felt intimidated.**
- ❖ **They may be annoyed or bored.**

Relationships, Duties, And Responsibilities

Relationships are an essential component of our identity. Relationships frequently change when someone has dementia. People suffering from dementia are prone to isolation and avoidance by others around them. They may lose contact with friends and relatives, who may be unsure how to respond to them.

As dementia worsens, some aspects of the relationship may become more difficult, such as a person's ability to care for people around them. However, many wonderful aspects of the relationship, such as affection, will continue. Caregivers and those around the person with dementia may find it beneficial to concentrate on these positive characteristics.

Fostering current relationships and encouraging the dementia patient to engage in social groups, neighborhood events, religious activities, or hobbies are two ways caregivers can support the patient. You can socialize with new people, have conversations about dementia, and take part in group activities in dementia cafés. Other social clubs can be learned about at the GP surgery, local library, or council office.

Caregivers and others can also contribute to fostering a dementia-friendly community. Because people in this community are aware of dementia, people with dementia can feel comfortable and actively participate in their communities.

Looking After Oneself

Dementia may also affect the person's relationships with those closest to them. A partner, friend, or child may find oneself identified as a caregiver. This is frequently an unintentional position, and many people do not consider themselves caregivers.

A caregiver may discover that they are taking on an increasing number of responsibilities in their relationship. While accepting greater responsibility may be essential, it is critical that the person with dementia continues to feel involved in and capable of contributing to the relationship.

Caregivers frequently have to balance the person's emotional demands with their own. For example, seeking replacement/respite care may be beneficial. A person with dementia may feel confused, nervous, or isolated if their primary caregiver is temporarily replaced by respite care, but it is also critical for carers to have time to rest and recover.

The Effects of Dementia on Individuals

The majority of people with dementia have memory and cognitive issues. This can cause loss of:

- ❖ **Self-esteem and Confidence**
- ❖ **Social roles and relationships.**
- ❖ **Ability to carry out hobbies**
- ❖ **Everyday life skills. For example, cooking and driving.**

However, the person will retain some of their abilities. Even later in the condition, they will maintain an emotional connection to others and their surroundings.

Dementia will disrupt a person's daily life. Caregivers can take steps to mitigate the effects of any changes and assist the individual in maintaining a sense of normalcy for as long as feasible.

Communicating

People with dementia frequently struggle to communicate, such as finding the proper word or keeping up with a conversation. Pain, other diseases, drug side effects, and sensory impairments are all potential barriers to communication.

Tips for caregivers on communication:

- *If the person has difficulty speaking, speak slowly and with simple words and sentences.*
- *A person with dementia may communicate using gestures, eye contact, and facial expressions.*
- *Attempt to keep eye contact. This will allow the person to focus on you.*
- *Avoid rapid movements and stiff facial expressions, as these can induce upset or anxiety.*
- *When speaking, avoid standing too close to or above someone; this can be threatening.*
- *Make sure the individual is included in conversations. Try not to speak on their behalf, finish their words, or let others exclude them.*
- *Listen to the individual. Give them plenty of time and eliminate distractions such as background noise. They may be attempting to transmit feelings rather than facts.*
- *Avoid posing too many inquiries. Consider providing options or asking yes/no questions.*

Independence

Families, friends, and caregivers should, if possible, encourage the person living with dementia to take care of themselves instead of 'taking over'. This improves the individual's well-being and helps them keep their dignity, confidence, and self-esteem.

Caregivers and others should avoid presuming the individual is unable to contribute or understand what is going on. The person should be as involved as possible. This can include allowing the person with dementia to do things in their own way, within reason. However, caregivers must strike a balance between independence and safety.

Tips for caretakers to keep independence

- ❖ ***Do things together; strive to do things with the person rather than for them.***
- ❖ ***Pay more attention to what the person is capable of than what they are not.***
- ❖ ***Allow plenty of time for tasks and provide reassurance and encouragement as needed.***
- ❖ ***Divide work into tiny steps.***
- ❖ ***Instead of focusing on the outcome of a task, consider the process.***

Maintaining a positive relationship.

The quality of life of the person with dementia is contingent upon the caregiver and the individual having dementia having a positive relationship. It is critical to discover solutions to continue the relationship. Tips for caregivers on relationships:

Instead of focusing on how things used to be, try to focus on the relationship as it is right now.

Think about techniques to improve your relationship, such as sharing hobbies, working on your life narrative, reflecting, and engaging in creative endeavors like music and painting.

If there are long-standing issues in the relationship, try to find ways to spend time apart, or investigate other forms of social assistance, such as a carers' support group or an online forum. You could also look into counseling and relationship support.

Don't be reluctant to talk to people about the changes in your relationship, whether they're friends, family members, or professionals like a therapist.

Decision-making

A person's ability to make their own decisions is referred to as mental capacity, or simply 'capacity'. It entails being able to weigh various possibilities, select one, and convey the outcome.

A person with dementia may gradually lose the ability to make certain decisions, such as financial ones, but it is usually presumed that a person has the capacity unless shown otherwise.

Any decision made for someone with dementia must be in their best interest. Decisions should be made using the least restrictive option and in accordance with the person's previously expressed wishes.

www.ingramcontent.com/pod-product-compliance
Lightning Source LLC
Chambersburg PA
CBHW051716250726

48653CB00007B/3064